Awake: Art of the Mississippi Delta

Emma Knowlton Lytle
December 3, 1910 - February 21, 2000

Awake
Art of the Mississippi Delta

Emma Knowlton Lytle

Publication: Spectrum Contemporary
ISBN-13:978-0-578-48148-7

 First edition, 2015. Second printing, 2019. Third printing, 2025.

AWAKE: ART OF THE MISSISSIPPI DELTA, BY EMMA KNOWLTON LYTLE

For Emma's Children, Nieces, Nephews —
Including all her Grand, Great-grand and Future Progeny —

In Celebration of Emma's Spirit and Creativity.

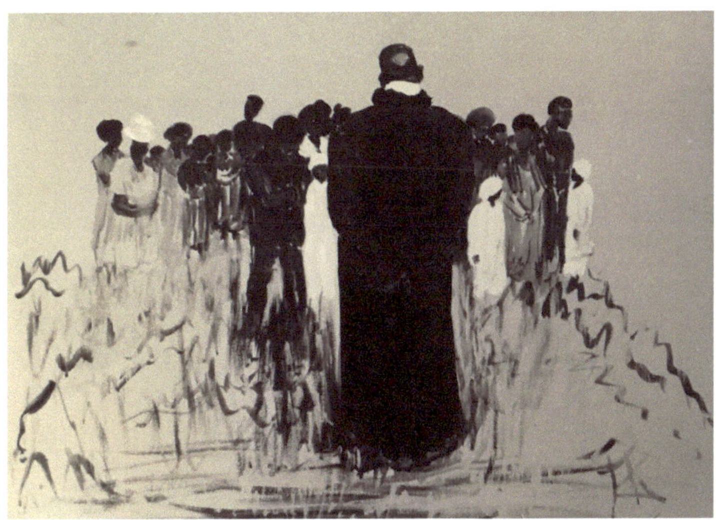

The Flock, Emma Knowlton Lytle

Author's Preface

My mother, Emma Knowlton Lytle, is the real author of this book. I have brought it to life to let her art speak with a minimum of additional narrative. Although this is just a sample of her vast body of work, I'm sure you will find her joy in creating and her message timeless.

The details of Mother's artwork and career are as accurate as her notes, letters, press permit; she would tell you she paid little attention to such things as dates, however, there are resources included in the back if you are interested in further research.

I would like to thank Cyndi Tolosa and Steven Lomazow for their tireless work and support over the many hours needed to put this together. Also, I am grateful to Carolyn Elkins and Terry Everett for their wonderful poems about Mother.

Suze Bienaimee
December 2015, New York City

Table of Contents

Artist Statement

These paintings, these sculptures and spin-offs from intimations that "once and future" is not an empty phrase, but the truth of individual being for everyone anywhere who is aware enough, awake enough.

Throughout my early life, schooling, marriages, motherhood, I would try some visual expression and then shy away from it. My vision was sure, my execution poor. In 1940 during my first widowhood, I began to pursue the needed skills.

Techniques can be taught and mastered. Meaning, if any, comes from soul, mind, heart. Significance is nurtured by the quality of life.

The visual, the vision comes from the invisible.

Emma Knowlton Lytle

Painting

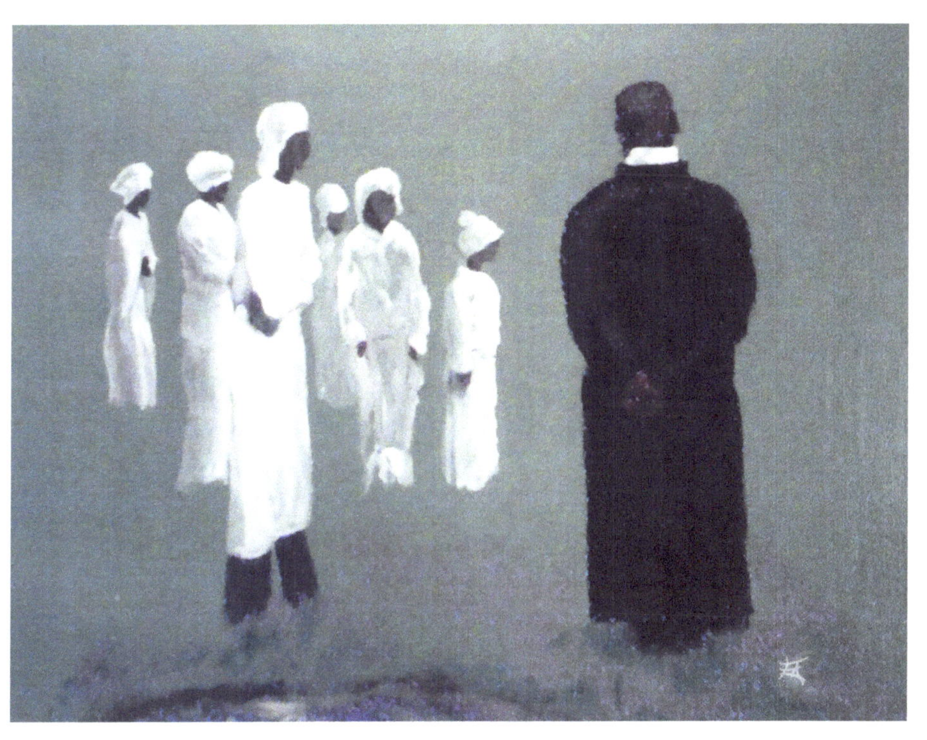

Our Father
46 x 42"
Emma Knowlton Lytle

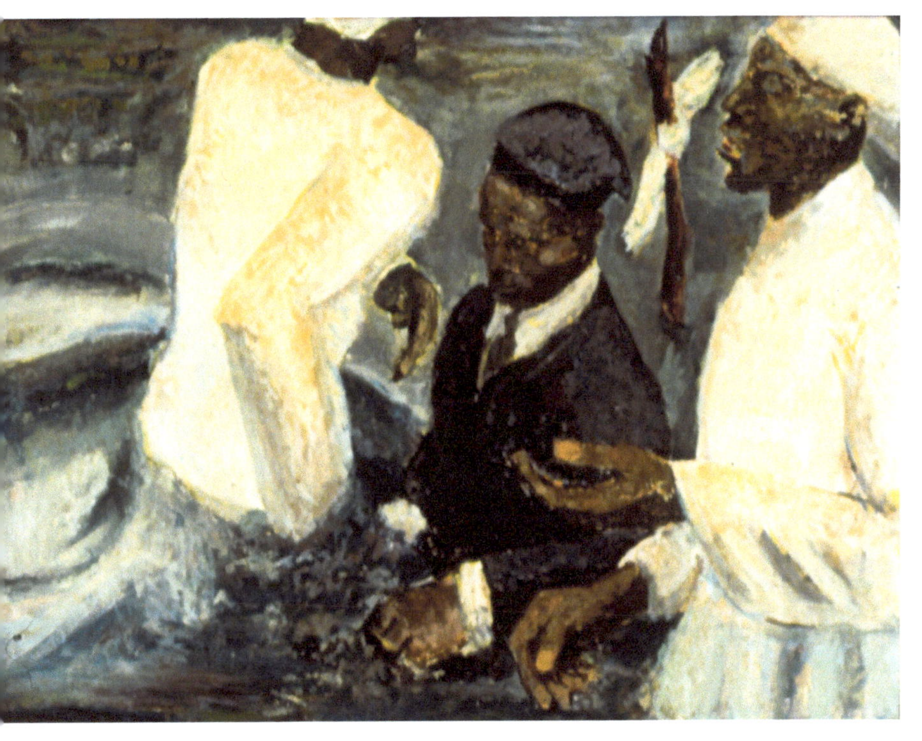

Our Father: Reverend Thomas Bronner and the Baptizers in the Bogue Phalia
46 x 42"
Emma Knowlton Lytle

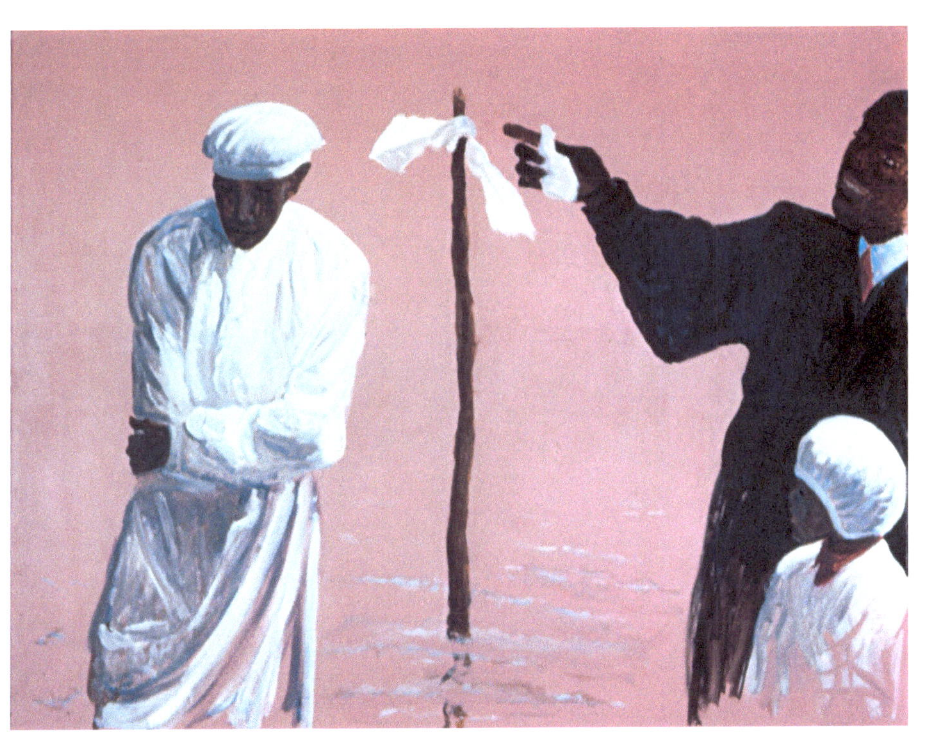

Silence is Louder
48 x 42"
Emma Knowlton Lytle

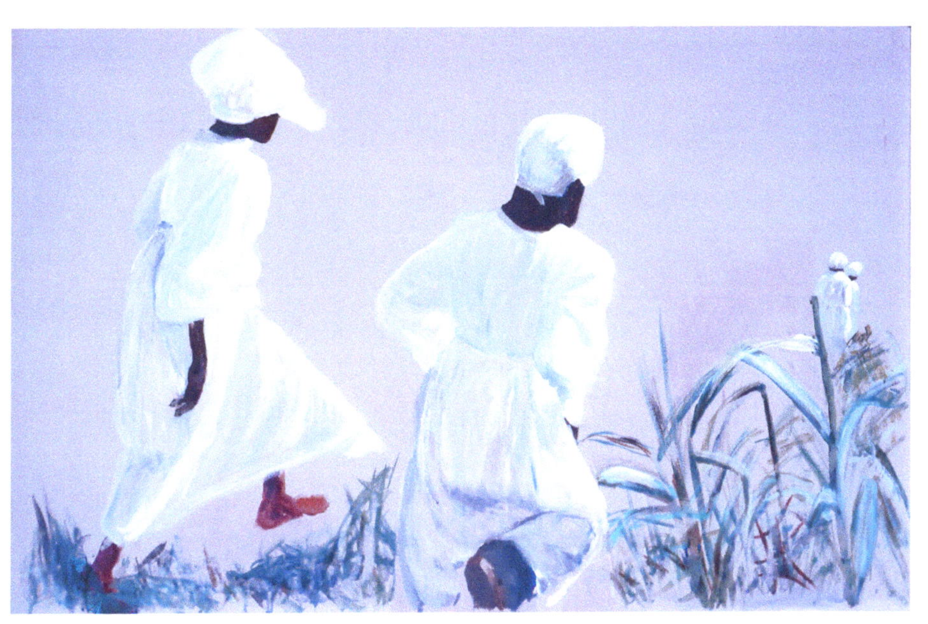

Glory Day
42 x 36"
Emma Knowlton Lytle

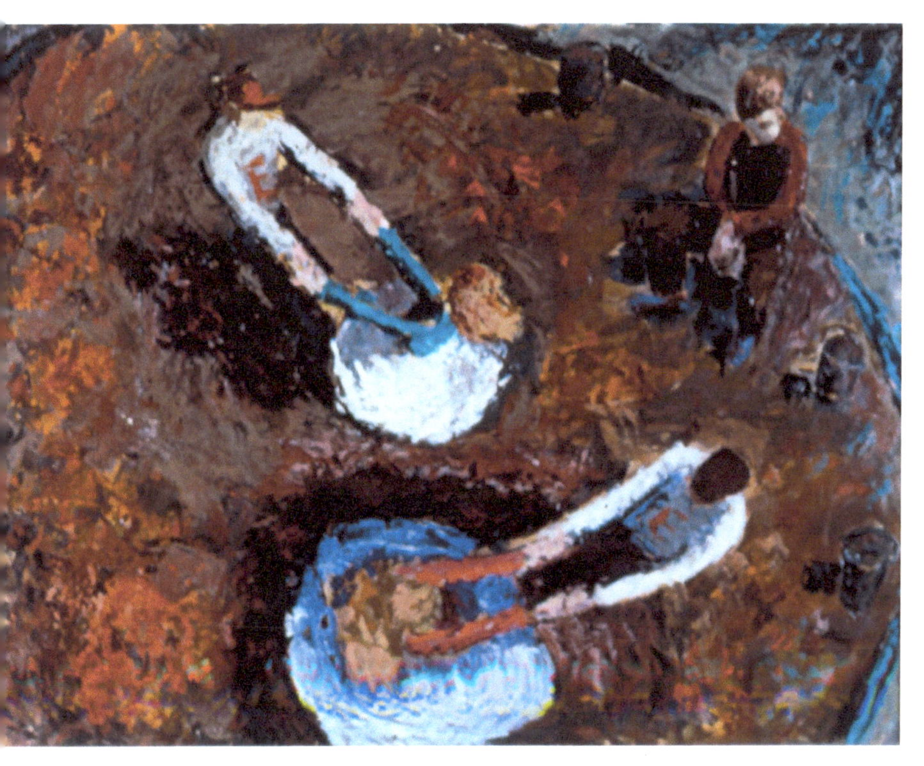

Wedding Overtones
40 x 36"
Emma Knowlton Lytle

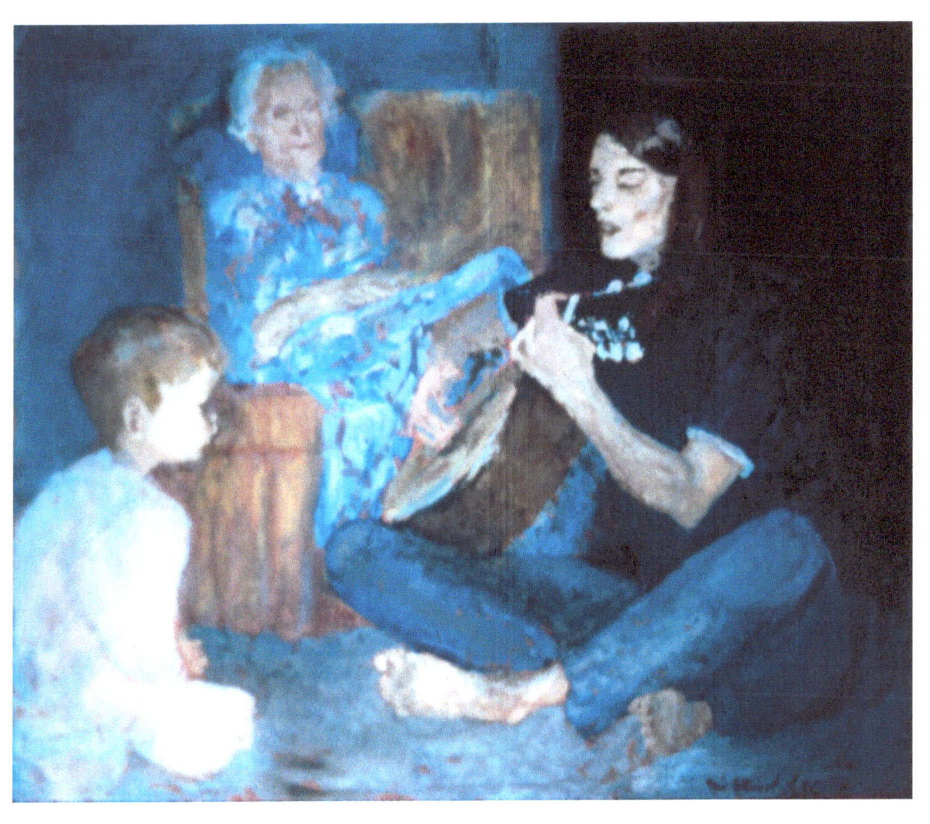

Three Generations
42 x 42"
Emma Knowlton Lytle

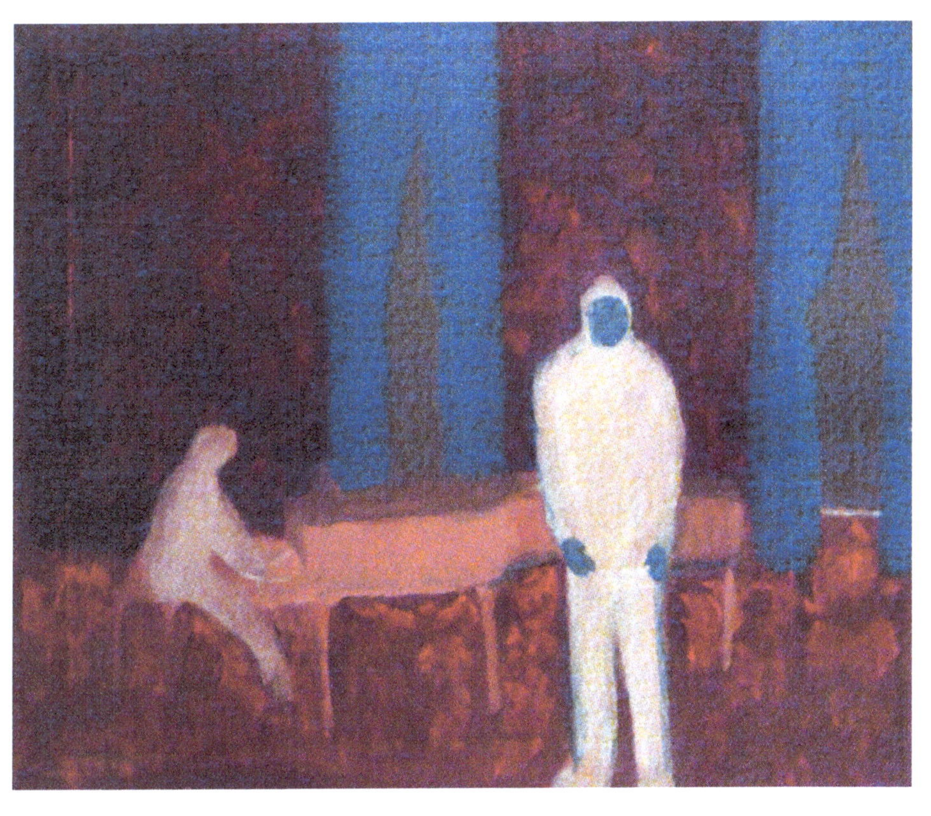

Opera Auditions: After Image II
18 x 24"
Emma Knowlton Lytle

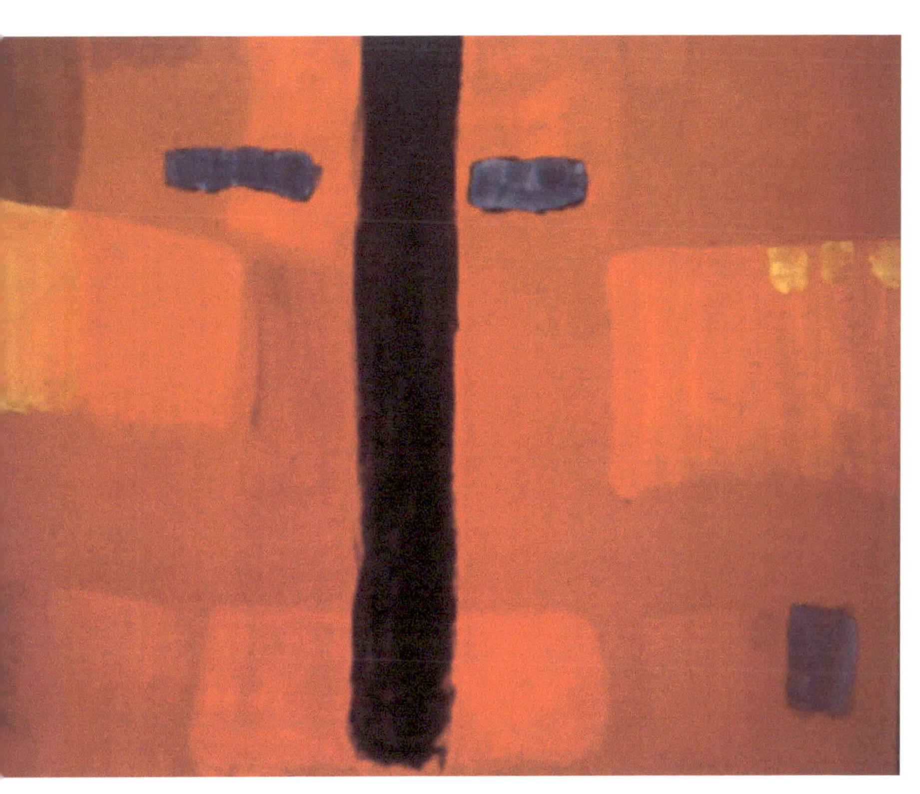

Clothesline Cross
42 x 36"
Emma Knowlton Lytle

Clothesline Red
42 x 36"
Emma Knowlton Lytle

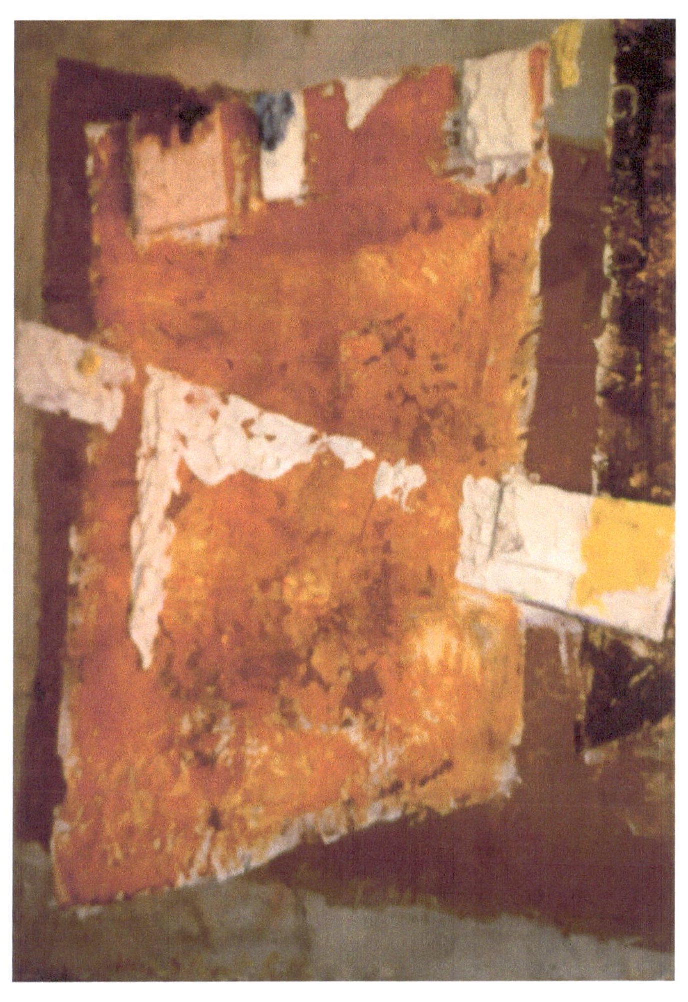

Clothesline
36 x 42"
Emma Knowlton Lytle

Sculpture

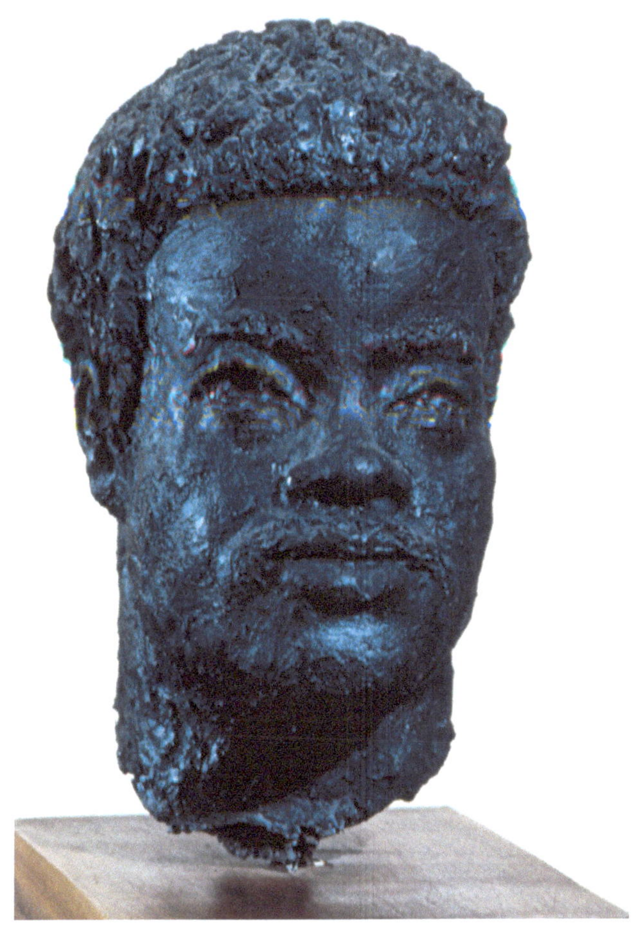

Henry
16" H
Emma Knowlton Lytle

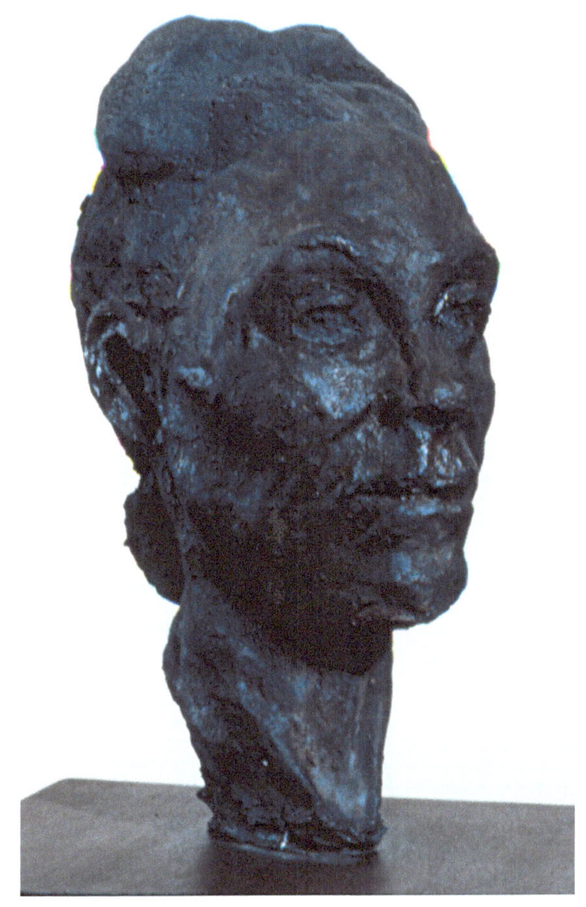

Georgia
17" H
Emma Knowlton Lytle

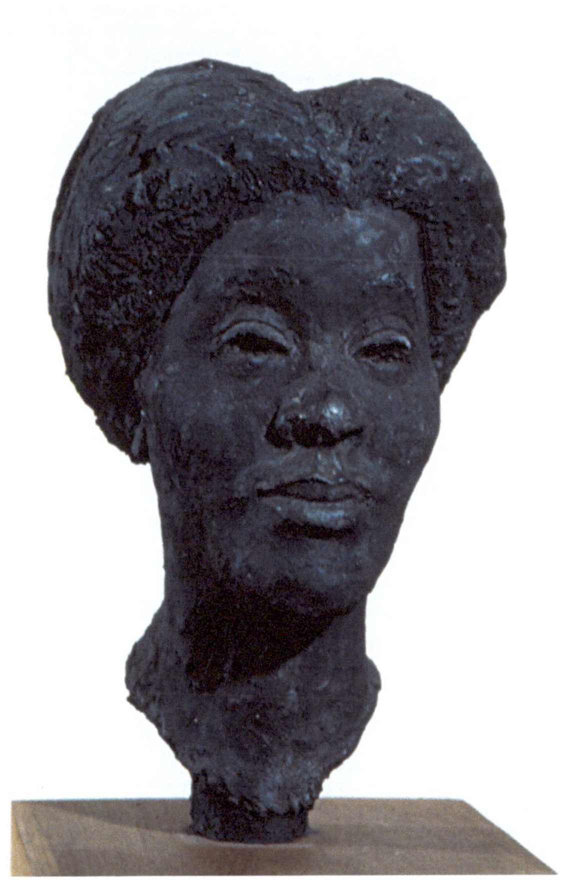

Arzilia
16" H
Emma Knowlton Lytle

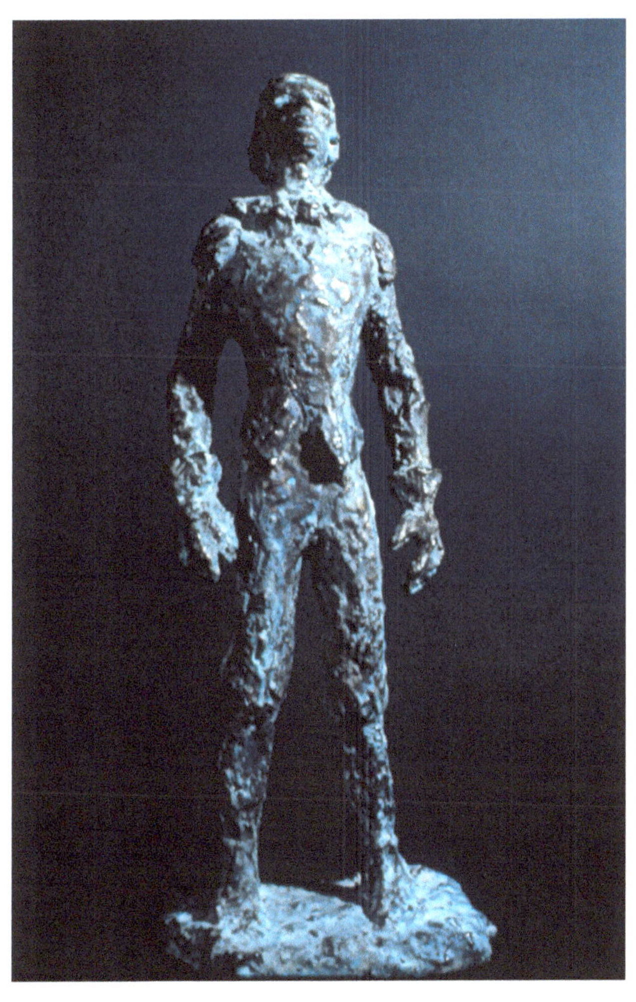

Brother Lawrence
24" H
Emma Knowlton Lytle

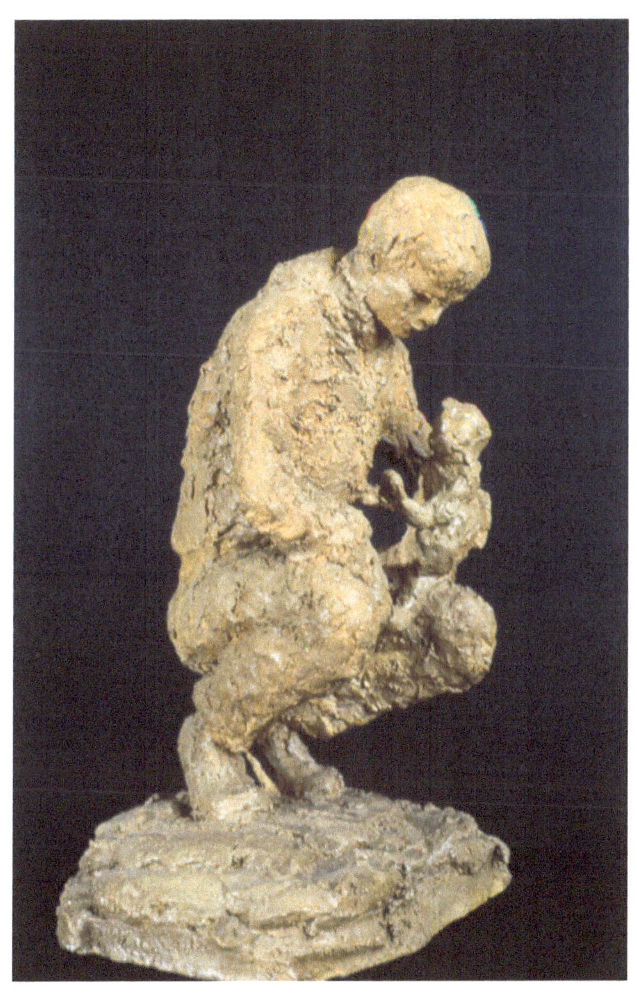

Father and Son
17" H
Emma Knowlton Lytle

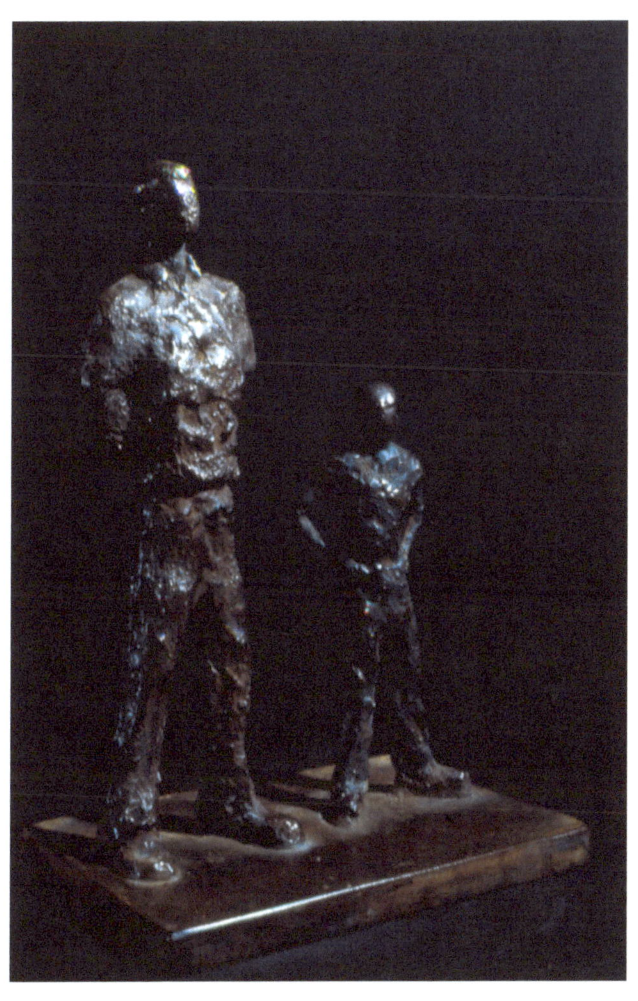

Father and Child
13" H
Emma Knowlton Lytle

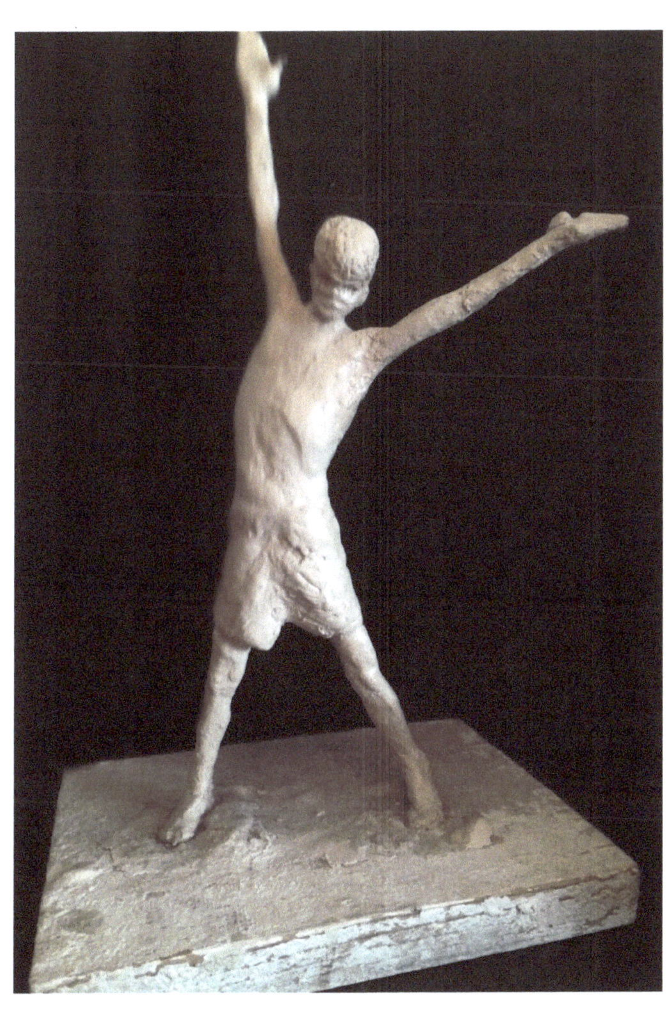

Robert, Cartwheel, Age 10
12" H
Emma Knowlton Lytle

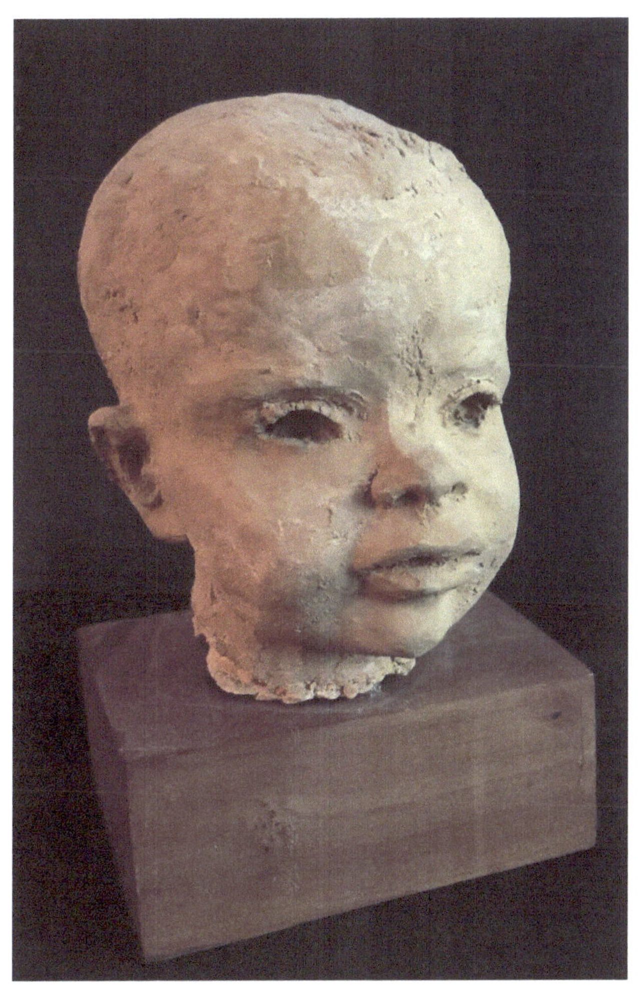

Robert, Infant
7" H
Emma Knowlton Lytle

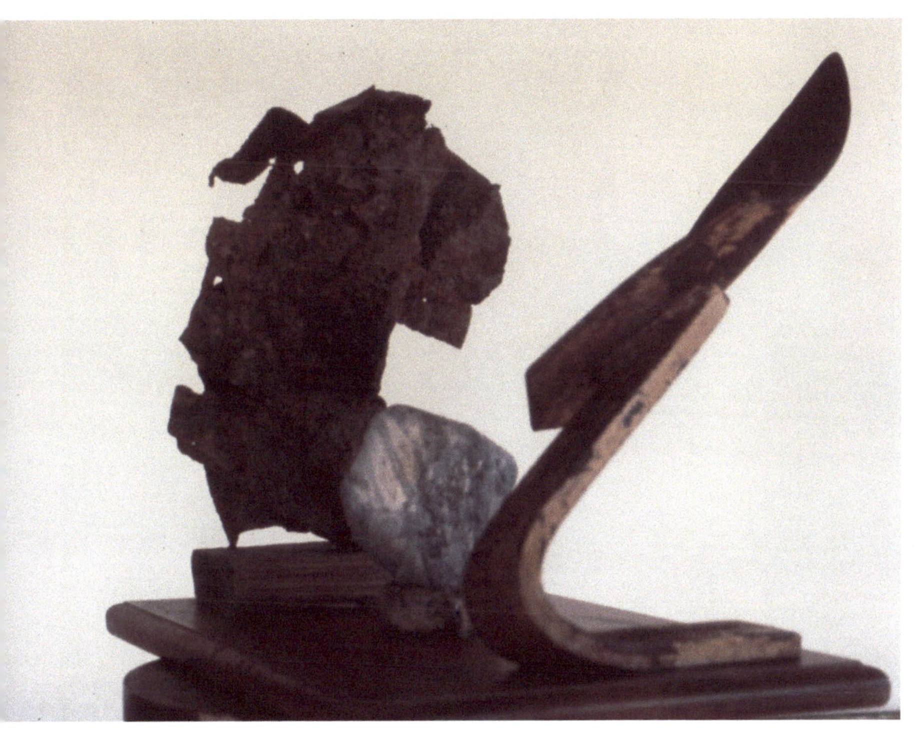

Assemblage
18" H
Emma Knowlton Lytle

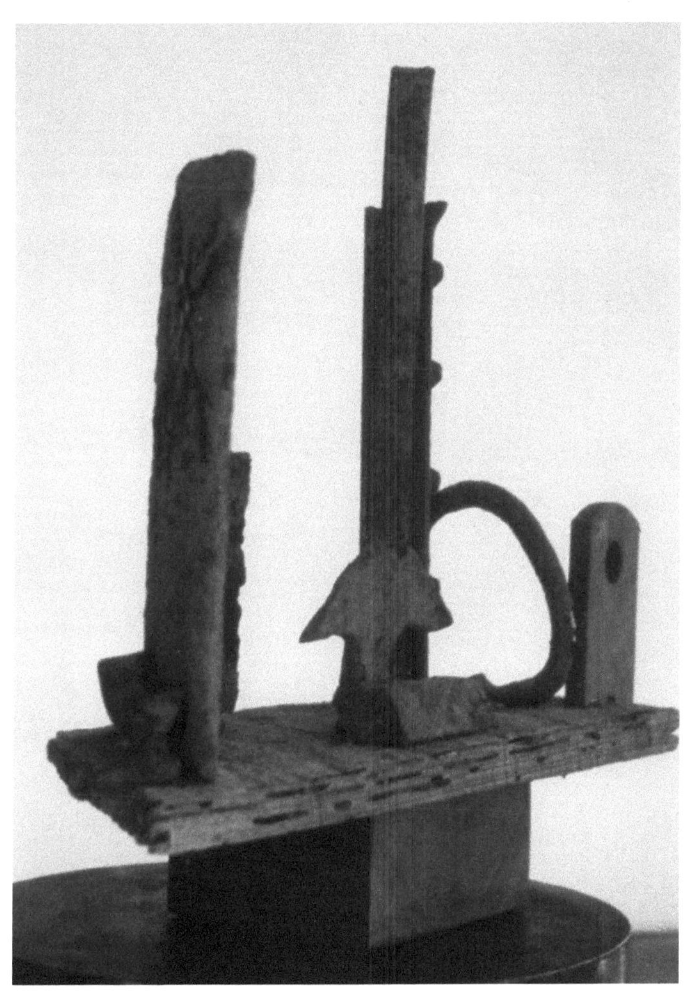

Assemblage
24" H
Emma Knowlton Lytle

Poetry

The Intent

Contrive a history of life, long poem
in sonnets, like a journal. Measured time,
recorded mystic thoughts, an infant Boehm
without question, listening to the chime,
the "Music of the Spheres", the peace within.

In color, warmth and comfort more than sin.
At this rested age no sin, no ploy
can tempt. The moment comes for thought,
and questions; memories too dim for care,
but some so vivid they become a part
of heaven and here. Can life add up to naught?
No, never true. The part that's lost I pare
too easily from thought. Now, therefore, I start.

Emma Knowlton Lytle
February 1984
From the Sonnet Series: *Bring Some Truth*

February 29, 1984

Pure narrative is difficult against
The sonnet form. It would not be so hard
If time itself were not beyond my strength
To sort, so memory could keep a card
Of each event timed chronologically.
The day to day details are mostly gone.
A residue of spirit is all I see
When I look back. I try to make a song,
A forward, to prepare the story's way,
To be in words some essence of all life,
That may for someone help to bring that day
Of understanding that alone ends strife.
Some day the strife may die within us all.
This day we must begin to lift the pall.

Emma Knowlton Lytle
From the Sonnet Series: *Bring Some Truth*

February 29, 1984

Warm scent of wood, the steady sound of clock,
The quiet of sitting still, the noise of boys —
The moment came, the silent taking stock,
Aware the stair seemed gossamer. My poise
Expanded, took within itself all time,
A bubble or balloon, eternal now —
I seemed to know without, within. Sublime
Peace I had and lost I knew not how.
Again upon the attic stair came fear,
The lost and dusty smell old ladies save
When all has passed them by and left no cheer
To warm them, no loving thoughts to lave
The torment of each year. I am not so.
As I live beyond four score and ten, I grow.

Emma Knowlton Lytle
From the Sonnet Series: *Bring Some Truth*

February 26, 27, 29, 1984

The fire, the tree, the stair, the earth all threads
That are repeated in my life and so
Will come to be important berths or treads
Where I, a child, on a stair, might bump aglow
With laughter down each step or sit bemused
In meditation, then, as now. Although
I did not know it then, I was infused
With dreams and visions that could bestow
On me a sense of knowing yet unused.
Long after on the stair the knowing came.
I'd had a ghostly image of the self
Grown-up. Awareness leaps beyond the bruised.
The child could not remain upon that shelf
But sought to know some life beyond the tame.

Emma Knowlton Lytle
From the Sonnet Series: *Bring Some Truth*

March 6, 1984

One morning early, barely, mostly bright
Before the day, before the sun, I woke.
Shaking back the covers to watch the smoke
Above the nearby homes I saw the night
No longer on the flat, the purple earth,
For mystery was making. Always before
I'd heard it said, I thought it well known lore,
"The sun rises" but here out of mist a birth
Of some experience that gave the lie
To that old word. In truth, I rode
The bed, the house, the world into that day
And found the dazzling sun, the clouds, the sky
No longer comforting as if I strode
Some new, some seamy path that led away.

Emma Knowlton Lytle
From the Sonnet Series: *Bring Some Truth*

March 14, 1984

The tree, magnolia tree, creates a mood.
Its arms, its branches, its ambience embraces,
Enfolds, inspires in me great fortitude.
I wonder if its growth, if time leaves traces
Of the numbers carved to mark my special seats
Where I would climb to have my world transformed —
The mast head of a giant ship that beats
Before the blow, or allied plane that stormed
Across the German lines in World War One —
Or my refuge for quiet and being still
In silence that would now, this year, become
A nourishing presence that delays the mill
Of time. The silence serves to obliterate
The score of ills, of sins, and scours all fate.

Emma Knowlton Lytle
From the Sonnet Series: *Bring Some Truth*

March 17, 1984

The hostler, "charioteer," of mules and wagon
Who made a trip each day to Perthshire store
Lived in Aunt Hennie's house some years, a score
Or more after her memory was gone
Or almost gone to others. Adventure was
The chance to ride with Alfred on the seat
And guide the mule's fast trot, to hear the creak
Of wheels, to feel teeth chatter like Christmas
Chill when heat on Delta land made sweat,
Mirage on the road and field looked like a flood
From broken levee. Distant trees submerged
Their roots. This was illusion but no threat
To that child's joy. Our children too have stood
By Alfred's side. More speed was always urged.

Emma Knowlton Lytle
From the Sonnet Series: *Bring Some Truth*

March 17, 1984

Some change is coming near. I walk the road
That skirts the bayou, now more a ditch than
A living stream as I remember it — broad
Where crawfish lined the bank. I'd scan
Each pellet home, a predator, in the mode
Of scouting beast. It took quick skill
To grab behind the huge claws and so avoid
A pinch. No mystic here, a hunter's kill
The target, every sense alert, deployed
To catch the wary creature. Once we cooked
The tails 'til burned and raw upon a stove
That was Aunt Polly's gift. She felt we rooked
Her for we let it later rust, her trove
She's saved for her own child who died so young.
We did not know from where her tears had sprung.

Emma Knowlton Lytle
From the Sonnet Series: *Bring Some Truth*

May 10, 1984

The tree, the cypress tree, that stood alone
Across the Bogue Phalia, became a lode,
A symbol of the peace within the bone
Of being, "the Word made flesh," a visual ode
To strength, to timelessness. All beauty stood
Before me. Green, the stream intervened.
The feel of the horse between my knees was good.
A time to watch the sun go by, time screened
To disappear. A warrior woman, Joan,
Became my heroine. I sought to seek
Her vision, found it futile to the tone
Of mind imbued with facts, the smells, the reek
Of droppings, all combined. I pulled the bit
And brought the horse away. Imagined it.

Emma Knowlton Lytle
From the Sonnet Series: *Bring Some Truth*

June 2, 1984

"To bind, to stretch, to dissipate the song"
Before the memories are too far away
As if to wonder did I get it wrong?
It matters not if one has found "The Way"
In contemplative silence — now to be
In time without the human need to plot
Its course. The fire, the earth, the stair, the tree
Remain. Not fear is left of death to blot
These days — no fear of life — for neither one
Can take away the Source of all my ways.
The chrysalis is open now, the web
Still catches light, is burnished still though spun
So long ago. My heart is filled with praise.
The balance is forever flow to ebb.

Emma Knowlton Lytle
From the Sonnet Series: *Bring Some Truth*

Admonition for a Poet

Magical, lyrical,
Lost in a blossomy pit;
Come coincide
On a mad ride.

Come pound.
Pound it out.
Spit leaves on the ground
But bring some truth about.

Emma Knowlton Lytle

Memory Scarcely Serves

So long ago we mothered our children in delight
her five, my three.

So long ago we shared our thoughts, our sense
of responsibility (public and private), our joys.

So long ago I knew a friend: beautiful, thoughtful,
steadfast, fired with faith: Lupe Reed.

A friend indeed.

Emma Knowlton Lytle

A Question

In wintered time
I am confounded by the stubborn deaf,
the deaf at heart.

In wintered time
the earth is flat, an ocean of dirt,
without response

to shadowed waves
that hold the message of all love
the body speaks.

In wintered time
the body, words and thoughts are still.

Is silence then a hearing aid to hearts?

Emma Knowlton Lytle

The Picnic

The fruit of many climes,
of many colors, painterly in its bowl.

The sandwiches a harmony
in white with accents brown and green.

And wine — golden wine.

The talk flowing, warm and
honest — of life — of conformity,
the need and burden of it.

The question: What is the infinite way?
the contemplative life?

The tree, magnolia tree embracing
sheltering, shading four of us.

The answer: there is something
to know — the unutterable.

Emma Knowlton Lytle

Is This Immortal?

How sparse the curtains of the soul
    that guard against the silence.
And yet we cling.

How keen the longing sigh.
    How can we hear one another?
And yet we cling.

How stark we really are —
    no place to hide.
And yet we cling.

Release the warmth of flesh
    (we must not cling)

Live — live now.

Eternally?

Emma Knowlton Lytle

Emma's Golden Road

It happened to her only a few times
though she used to drive a lot. She came around
that corner that moved the low sun
from where it had been
riding in her side window
to shining down her back
and straight on through her,
turning the long road ahead
into sudden gold. And once —
a ride she still goes down in dreams —
the road in front was rising
into low hills, and the rain
had made the blacktop shine
so that the sun behind and the road
and hills and sky ahead, all
became one fire
through which she seemed to fly
out from the sun
shooting across radiant space
on an infinite stream of light.
The universe seemed what it must be
then, a journey instead of a place,
a road she had yet to set out on,
and had long ago been down.

Carolyn Elkins
for Emma

Emma's Song

She in whom the Word resides, Emma,
looks daily across green fields or brown
into gray and rosy dawns,
into blue mornings and afternoons,
into azure noons and orange suns pulling
down the purple dusks that linger long
in this Delta where the level land
stretches to make this faraway country
she has loved long and well, and with her hands
out of the light she sees, out of the light she is,
she makes a veiled woman dance on canvas,
or an "I" stretch beyond the stratosphere,
or a bust be forever in bronze,
or a group gather for the last time
and yet forever in the canvas water
Blacks in white robes for outdoor baptism,
or a robin run across the page
of one of her aubades or sonnets.
She in whom the Word resides: Emma.

Terry Everett
for Emma

I wrote the following poem in 1993 to celebrate Mother. She pushed back against the norm to create her art and her life — to create her artistic gifts for all of us and these gifts are to live what you believe, live in love, practice forgiveness. She knew we are all one people, in one world.

The Best

I always thought she could
scream at the gods
the best. She has to as a woman
and an artist.

In the studio, in the fields,
on a soapbox, behind a lectern,
at the ballot box. How else
could she tuck potency

into a near century of life,
path finding? In walking the Delta
fields, silence collides with wind,
roar blurs land and sky. She sees.

Hears. Sun starches green to white.
In her studio her palette
the spectrum of eternity. Chisels.
Film, photographs, paintings. Colors

piled in time immediate,
all time. Brushes radiating
possibility. Transforming.
Vision.

Art to change
your mind, your heart.
Paradox. Giving. Black
on white. Awake and always poised.

Suze Bienaimee
for Mother

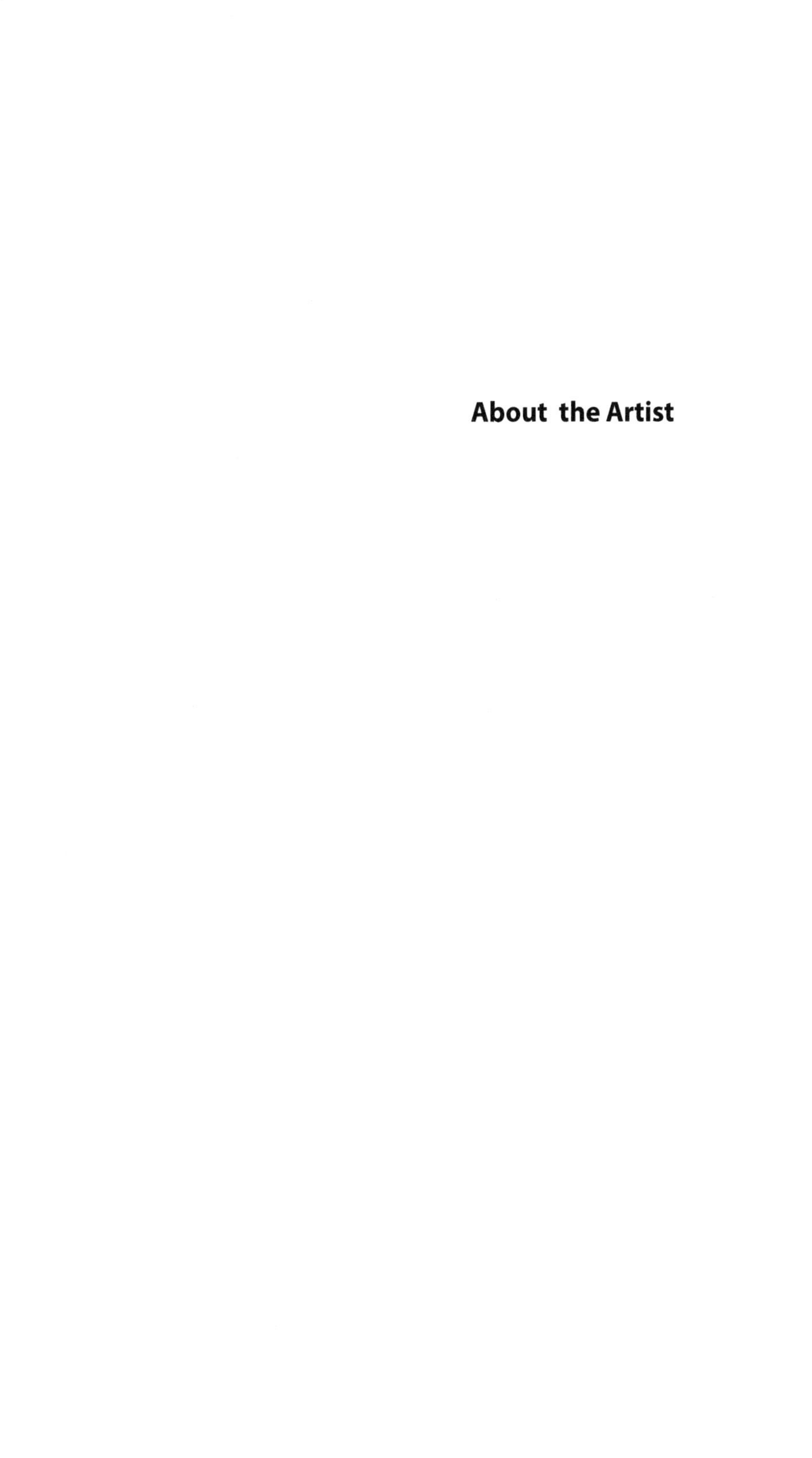

About the Artist

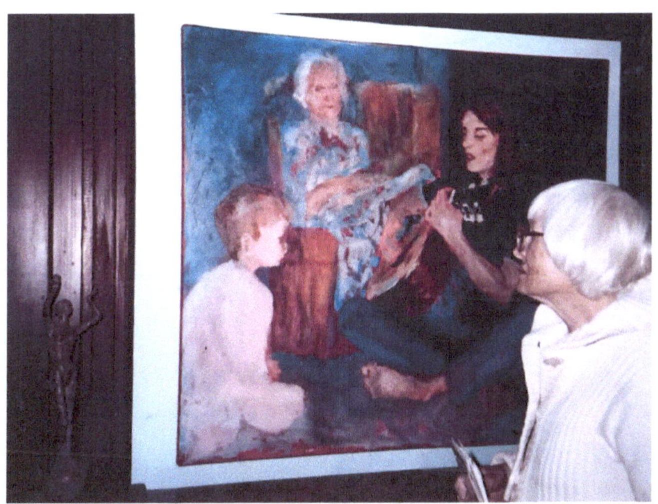

Left to right: *Maturity* sculpture; *Three Generations* painting (artist's granddaughter Liza, mother Susie, daughter Suze); artist, Emma Knowlton Lytle

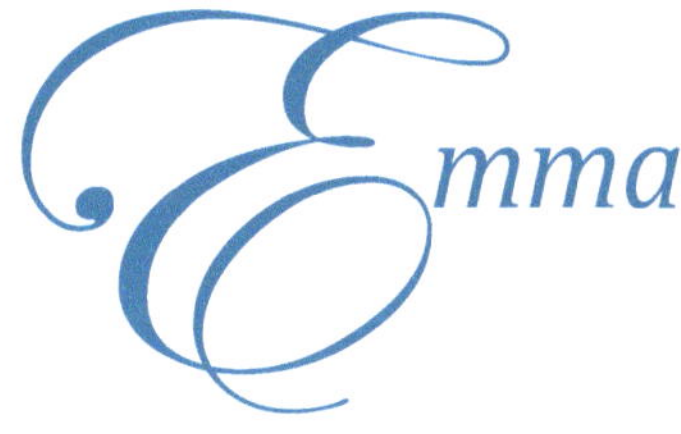

Emma

Emma Knowlton Lytle lived life devoted to art, creativity and communication.

The range of her artwork includes painting, sculpture, film, photographs and poetry; all were used to record life in her native Mississippi Delta and to give a voice to her deep convictions. She was a pathfinder, peacemaker and mystic in the sense that her deep reverence for all life — Black and white — was reflected in not only her daily actions, but through her artwork.

The Baptism paintings became possible because of her trusted and lifelong friendship with Reverend Thomas Bronner. Over the years he invited her to attend his church baptisms on Stamps Lake and the Bogue Phalia in Perthshire, Mississippi. The bronze portrait sculptures

depict Delta citizens, friends, family, faith; the Assemblage sculptures were created from abandoned and broken farm equipment found in the fields; the Clothesline paintings were inspired by colorful clothes drying on lines across the Delta and then transformed into abstract symbols of faith. The selection of Lytle's poems included range from free-verse to some from her sonnet series, *Bring Some Truth*. Her stated goal in the series was to write her life story in sonnets like a journal.

Lytle's award winning documentary films, *Raising Cotton* and *Mule Races*, (1938 – 1941), are now preserved as part of the Southern Media Archives in the Center for Southern Culture at the University of Mississippi at Oxford. They also received honors from the Women's Film Restoration Fund. *Raising Cotton* was shown at the prestigious Tribeca Film Festival, New York City in 2011.

Lytle exhibited widely in juried exhibitions: the Annual of the Art Institute, Chicago, Illinois, 1957 and in the Artist Members Exhibit of Pen Women, Mississippi Competition, 1985, Greenwood, Mississippi. Lytle received first place awards in several juried exhibitions: National League of American Pen Women Mid-administration Show, 1983; Cottonlandia Museum Competition, 1984,

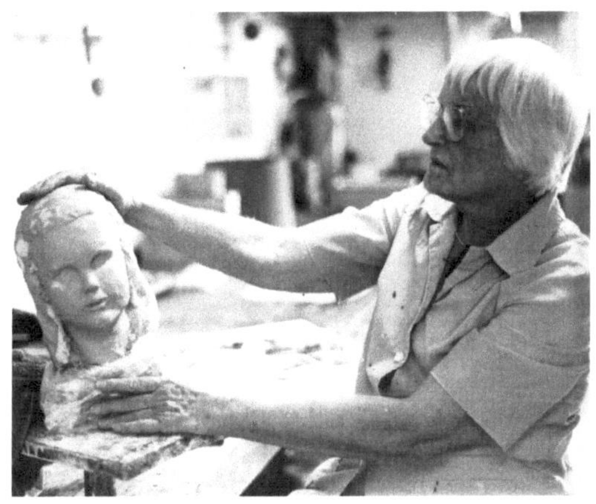

Artist at work

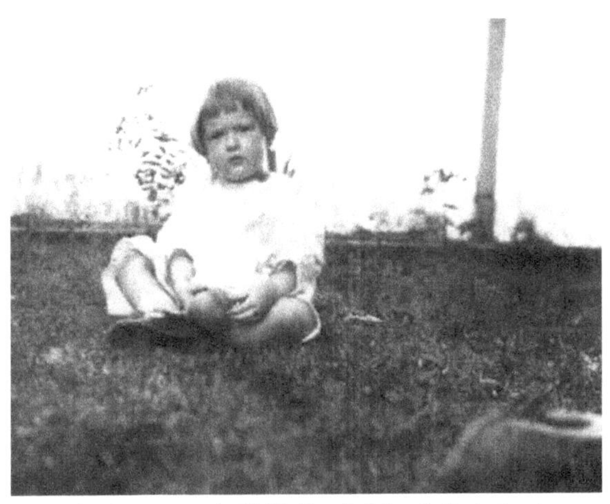

Artist at age 4, 1915, Perthshire, Mississippi

(*Glory Day*, page 13); the Trustmark of Greenwood Award, 1987, (*Father and Son*, page 37). Please note some of these artworks are a part of the permanent collection of Cottonlandia Museum — now named Museum of the Mississippi Delta, Greenwood, Mississippi.

Her solo exhibitions included: The Center for the Study of Southern Culture, University of Mississippi, Oxford, 1982; Delta State University, Cleveland, Mississippi, 1986 and 2000.

A Magna Cum Laude graduate of Radcliffe (Harvard) College, 1932, Cambridge, Massachusetts, in Law and International Relations, Lytle's career as an artist began almost a decade later in the 1940s when she first studied painting with George Parker in Massachusetts, took miscellaneous classes at the Dallas Art Institute and then sculpture with Leon Koury in Greenville, Mississippi. In 1945 she also studied at the Art Institute of Chicago in Chicago, Illinois.

Lytle was married to Jack Rose Humphreys of Greenwood, Mississippi until widowed in 1940. In 1945 she married Stuart Bruce Lytle of Chicago, Illinois. She was the mother of three (Eleanor, Robert, Suze) and the grandmother of five.

Emma Lytle was also honored at the *Sesquicentennial Celebration of Bolivar County, Mississippi*, June 29, 1986, Great River Road State Park, Rosedale, Mississippi as Honorary Artist of Bolivar County.

Given a lifetime of inspiration initially sparked as a child when she saw original art for the first time, Lytle wanted to share this experience with her fellow Mississippi Delta residents, especially children. She created an ambitious program and shared her art and that of other artists by mounting exhibits in even the tiniest Delta town libraries such as Shelby, Drew, and Gunnison.

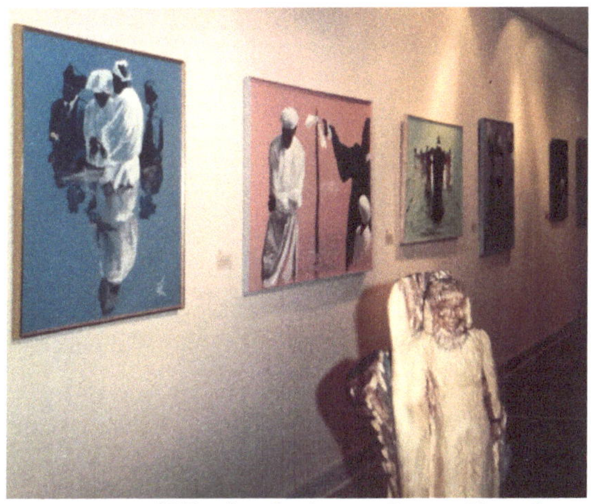

Baptisms and Wooden Sculpture, Emma Knowlton Lytle, Exhibition, Delta State University, 1986

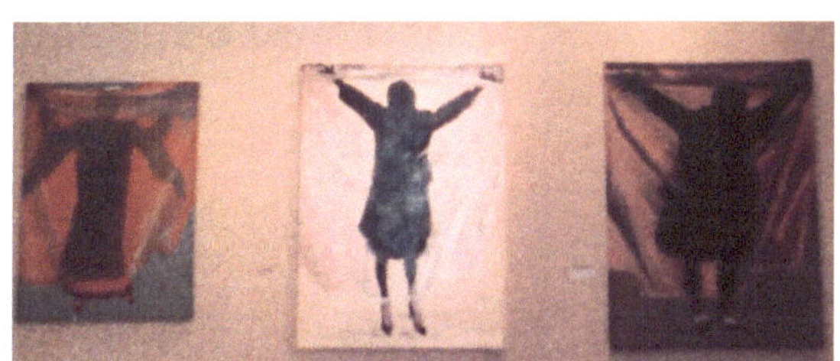

Clothesline, Emma Knowlton Lytle, Exhibition, Delta State University, 1986

Rachel Brown's article in the *Bolivar Commercial* in September of 1987, "Women I'd Love To Be Like" featured Emma Lytle:

A free spirit. Creative. Vivid. Fearless.
Full of ineffable secrets.
Proprietor to a mysterious fountain of youth.
Forward looking. Self-aware. Intelligent.
An earthly pilgrim in search of heavenly Truth.
On canvas and in sculpture, for years she has recorded
the deceptively mundane events
of the countryside surrounding her home.
With a keen eye of an out-of-town reporter
she plucks a moment
from time and gives it shape and form.
Her renderings of the Stamps Lake baptizings
have immortalized a tradition of Black Delta life.

"The real adventure of life", *she says,* "is in your mind."

Transparent. Enigmatic. I want to be like Emma Lytle...

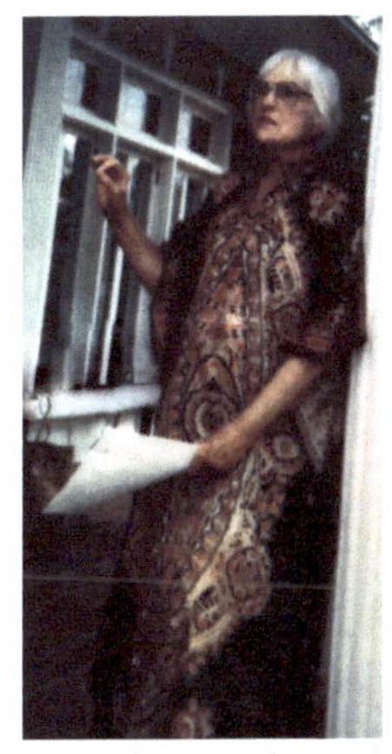

Emma Knowlton Lytle reading her poetry, Perthshire, Mississippi

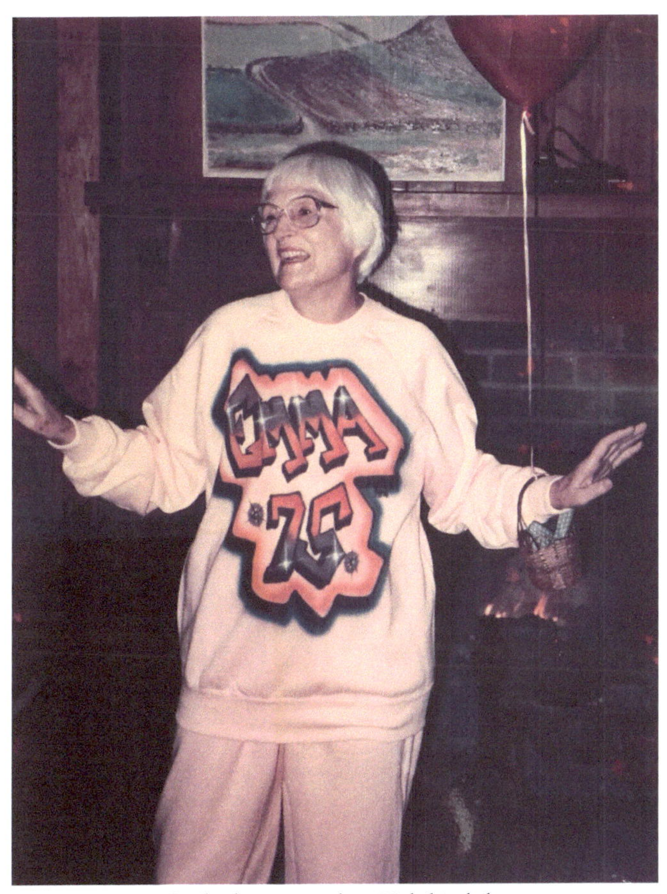

Emma Lytle dancing at her 75th birthday party

Resources

MississippiEmma.com

Gibert, Knowlton, Lytle Family Archive, Delta State University, Cleveland, Mississippi

Mississippi Roads Educational TV, Three Programs: Emma Knowlton Lytle Interview in 1988; "Baptism", 1980s; "Rev. Thomas Bronner of Bethel Church, Perthshire, Mississippi", 1980s.

Center for Southern Culture, University of Mississippi, Oxford Mississippi

Art Index

Paintings

Sculptures

EKL: Emma Knowlton Lytle's
initials and artistic signature

Emma Knowlton Lytle's
personal signature

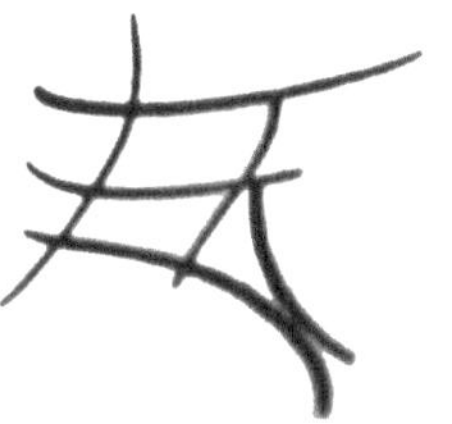

LOVE

Janma

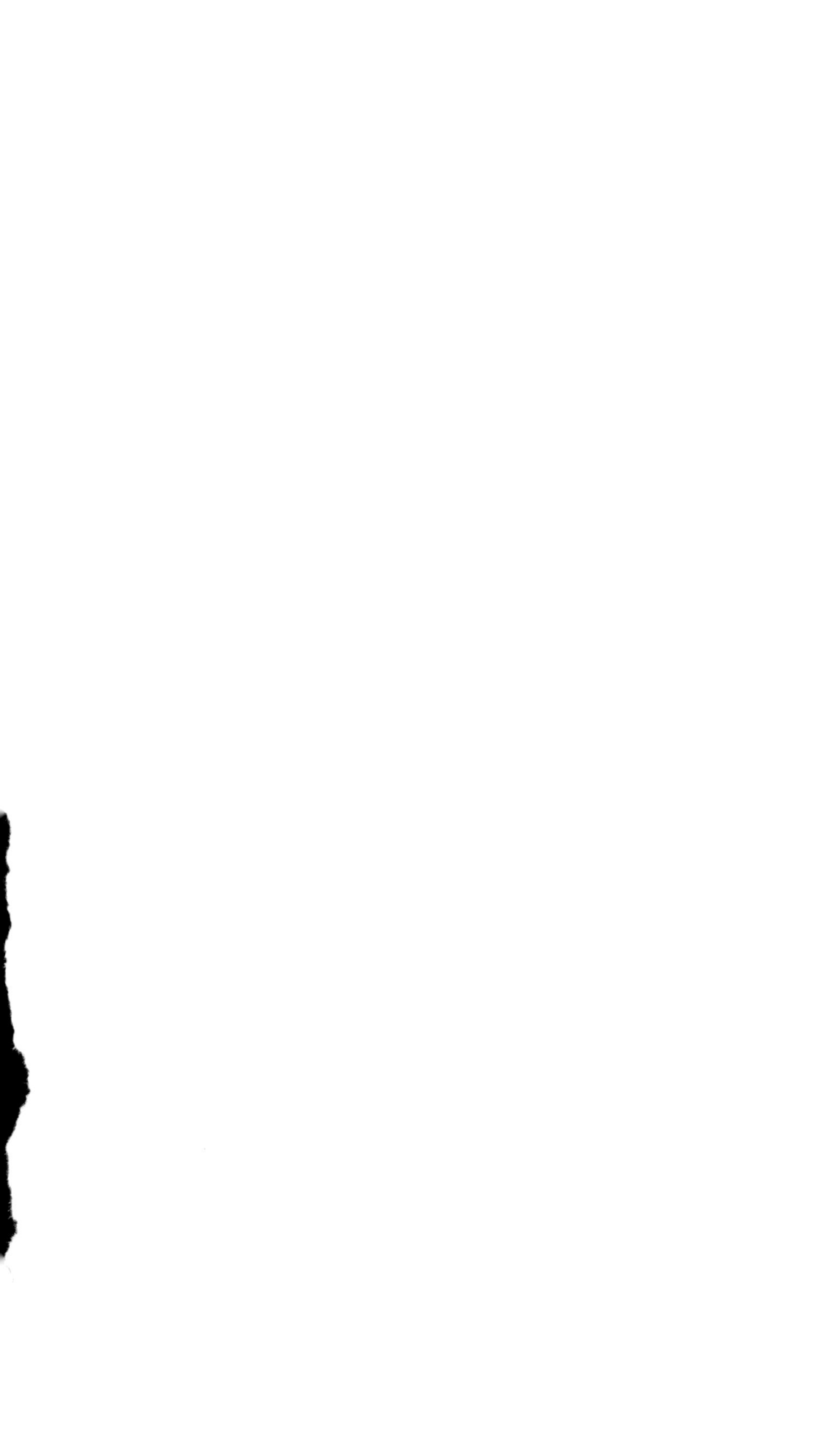

www.ingramcontent.com/pod-product-compliance
Lightning Source LLC
LaVergne TN
LVHW052307100826
845147LV00006B/691

* 9 7 8 0 5 7 8 4 8 1 4 8 7 *